GW01605581

Many years ago, Timsgaard was the richest estate in all Jutland. In its great manor house, built by the powerful squire, Peder Guildenstiern, lived *Tim the nisse*, a small mischievous creature who has the power to keep the estate happy and prosperous.

Our adventure begins with the arrival of Sorn, the new farm hand, who on his first night outwits the nisse. Sorn strikes a bargain with Tim to help him with his farm work, the threshing, haymaking and ploughing.

After a savage encounter between Tim and the wicked nisse Tam, the story ends happily for Sorn and for Tim, if not for the Squire and his estate.

Ib Spang Olsen's illustrations capture all the impish humour of these folk tale characters and the atmosphere of traditional farm life in Denmark.

THE NISSE FROM TIMSGAARD

illustrated by

Ib Spang Olsen

Retold by Virginia Allen Jensen
from a story by Vilhelm Bergsøe

Angus & Robertson Publishers

Angus & Robertson Publishers
London . Sydney . Melbourne . Singapore
Manila

First published by Angus & Robertson Publishers (UK) Ltd. in 1974
Reprinted 1976

National Library of Australia
card number and ISBN 0 207 95547 6

Printed in Hong Kong

To that little grey man
whom I met in the barn long ago

What Is A Nisse?

When you have read this story, you will *know* what a nisse is!

Now, before you begin, you may have guessed that the little, old, gruff-bearded fellow wearing a red cap is a nisse. His name is Tim. Tim may look as if he should be called something else—an elf, a goblin, a gnome, or a dwarf. He is related to these creatures, but he is not quite the same. He *is* a nisse, and he lives in Denmark. It can't be said exactly where he lives now, although it is known that he lived at Timsgaard about four hundred years ago and that Timsgaard has had bad luck ever since he moved away.

A nisse is small, but he is strong; he is very, very old and gnarled, yet agile. He is unassuming when he is treated well, but he becomes grumpy and even dangerous when disregarded. Sometimes he is merry or just plain mischievous. He has amazing powers and some limitations. Occasionally he allows himself to be seen—when he removes his cap or when a person understands him and makes friends with him. He can also be seen when a piece of iron is cast in his direction.

Few people know real nisser any more, but in the old days there was a nisse on almost every Danish farm. People know when a nisse is around even though he is invisible most of the time. They know that they must treat him with respect. For one thing, each evening they must set out a bowl of porridge for him with a lump of fresh butter in it. If they don't, there's no telling what treacherous tricks the nisse might play on them. But if they respect him and meet his simple needs, the nisse will take good care of everything on the farm and he will protect it from nisser on the other farms.

As long as nisser have lived in Denmark—and that is for hundreds and hundreds of years—people have told stories about their encounters with them. Vilhelm Bergsøe knew these stories, and he himself told this one about Tim from Timsgaard.

The manor house has long since been torn down and the west wind has had free play over the moat for many, many years, but in the old days Timsgaard was one of the greatest and richest estates in all Jutland. The manor house was built by Peder Guildenstiern, a squire who was so powerful that he dared overtake the King on the way to church and say "Pooh!" as he passed. He built the manor house in a marsh just to make it cost as much as possible, but even so, it was magnificent.

A nisse lived on Timsgaard, and I can tell you that he was about the sharpest nisse in all the land. It was mainly due to him that gold coins always covered the bottom of the Guildenstierns' coffer no matter how foolishly they spent their money.

The servants at Timsgaard were careful to attend him properly. Each evening they climbed to the top of the east tower and entered a small octagonal room furnished with a cot, a chair, and a porringer.

They poured a quart of porridge into the porringer and placed a lump of butter in it. The lump of butter was not to be forgotten. That would anger the nisse. Each morning they made up the cot with fresh straw, for that is how the nisse wanted it. They never saw him, but no matter how securely they locked the door of the room in the evening, each morning they found the porringer empty and a hollow in the middle of the cot where the straw was matted down as if a cat had been sleeping there.

One year towards the end of September, about the time of Michaelmas, the squire was expecting a new head carl to take charge of the work in the fields. He turned up towards midnight and reported to the steward.

"I'm the new head carl," he said. "My name is Sorn."

"What are you thinking of, arriving at such an hour!" the steward said peevishly. "Timsgaard is filled with guests for the hunt, and I have to house their servants in my own quarters. The only place left where there's space enough to swing a cat is the nisse's room."

"That's good enough for me," Sorn said.

"Then you don't know Tim of Timsgaard," the steward replied. "He can make himself as small as a flea; but if he gets angry, he might take it into his head to rub you down with the harrow! If you disturb his rest, he'll pitch you out of the tower."

"Ah, it won't come to anything so foul as that," Sorn said. "I have met nisser before, and I have my own way of dealing with them. Truthfully, I have been good friends with all the nisser I have ever known."

"Well, don't say I didn't warn you," the steward said. "It's your own hide. Here's the key. The room is in the east tower and the entrance is near the cellar door."

Sorn fumbled his way up the spiral staircase to the top of the tower, where he found a little door. The key fitted the lock. There was so little light inside the room that he could barely make out the cot, the chair, and the porringer.

Sorn was careful not to touch the porringer, but he took the feather bedding and the pillow from the cot, leaving only the fresh straw. He shook the straw and fluffed it up well in the middle of the cot. Under the eaves he made a soft bed for himself with the feather bedding and he propped the pillow up against the wall. Then he removed his leather breeches, rolled them up in the shape of a cone, and placed them on the chair next to the cot. He crawled into his bed, said his prayers, and being tired from his long journey, he soon fell asleep, even though the covers were too short for him.

Just as the watchman in the courtyard below cried "Twelve o'clock!" Sorn was awakened by the sound of the door at the foot of the tower opening and banging shut. Something was moving slowly up the stairs, wheezing and groaning like an old man barely able to lift his feet from step to step. When it reached the door of the room, it seemed to stand still, gasping frightfully for breath.

Suddenly it was in the room, rattling the porringer. Then Sorn knew what it was. He moved slightly to get a better look without being seen himself, but he could see nothing in the dim light coming through the windows.

It was still rattling the porringer. Sorn heard it jab the spoon into the butter hole and then dash the spoon abruptly to the floor. An angry voice said:

"The porridge is burned,
The butter has turned.
Those slovenly maids should be thrashed!"

"Ay, they have it coming!" Sorn said.

Suddenly it was quiet near the porringer.

A moment later there was a rustling, a prowling, and a cat-like spitting near the bed. Sorn lay still, even when he felt something crawl over him several times. The voice hissed:

"Gloom, leave the moon!
Its light is wretched,
Its light is wretched."

"You should polish it with pumice instead of pummelling me with your feet here in the dark," Sorn said.

At that very moment the moon came out from behind the clouds and clear rays of light shot through the windows. Sorn saw an old, grey-haired creature staring intently at the leather breeches and holding his pointed red cap in his hands. He was comparing the size of his cap with the roll of leather on the chair. The nisse was so preoccupied with measuring the breeches that he failed to see Sorn.

"Now how can I use that?
A cap? a hood? a hat?"

He picked up the breeches, put them on his head, and buttoned them under his chin. Then he yanked them off and snarled:

"This piece of hide's no good
For cap or hat or hood!"

"A pox on you!" Sorn said in a loud voice. "You're a slow fox, you are, if at your age you don't know a pair of leather breeches when you see them."

"Leather breeches?" the nisse asked. "What are they for?"

"Here, I'll show you," Sorn said. He got out of bed and put them

on. "See, they're not for your head, they're for your legs. This pair can last a man all his life."

The nisse danced around the strapping young carl and watched in amazement how he buttoned the breeches and bound them at his knees and his waist. When Sorn finished dressing, the nisse ran his hands down his own legs and said, "Sure as I'm Tim, I'd like to have those breeches. Can you get along without them?"

"This is my only pair. You cannot have them, but you may borrow them at night while I'm asleep."

"If only I can get into them," the nisse said.

"There are many ways to make them fit," Sorn said. "Jump on to the chair and I'll help you."

The nisse was up on the chair and waiting impatiently before Sorn got out of the breeches. Sorn held them out, saying, "Put one leg in this hole . . . and the other one in that hole."

So eager was Tim to get into the breeches that he sprang in with both legs at once, and there he hung astride the crotch, unable to reach the floor with his feet. Quickly Sorn buttoned the breeches under his chin and pulled the belt tight around his neck.

"Now, no matter what you do, you can't get out unless I loosen the breeches." And with that Sorn crossed the nisse twice.

Tim flew into a rage. Oh, how he carried on! He stamped and kicked, he turned somersaults and stood on his head, but he couldn't get out of the breeches for they were double-stitched by the best tailor in Ringkøbing.

Finally, he grew tired and implored Sorn to loosen the breeches and let him out.

"If you'll make a bargain with me," Sorn said, "I'll let you out."

"No!" the nisse cried. "I'm too old to bargain. These breeches will split before I bargain with you." Tim sprang so wildly about the room that Sorn feared he would fly straight through a window.

At last, Tim gave in. He collapsed breathlessly on the floor, rolled over to the foot of the chair and whimpered, "All right, I'll bargain with you, but don't make shameless demands of me."

"I won't," Sorn said. "Now listen. First of all, you must share this room with me. You'll sleep on the cot and I'll sleep on the floor."

"That's nice of you," the nisse said. "The floor is very hard."

"Second, I'll make sure that the quart of porridge served to you each evening is exactly as you like it, that it's never burned and the butter never rancid."

"If that's what you call bargaining," the nisse said, "then let's bargain some more. Go on!"

"Good," Sorn said. He went on. "Third, all I ask of you is that you come whenever I whistle, and help me with whatever I ask."

"Is that all?"

"Yes, that's all."

"You should have said so in the first place. I like this bargain. I'm glad you made it with me and not with that knavish nisse at Tamstrup Manor." Tim thought for a moment. "Wait," he said, "part of the bargain must be that you wear those breeches to bed every night. I never want to lay eyes on them again."

Sorn loosened the breeches and the nisse crawled up on the bed of bare straw. Sorn put the breeches on and went to sleep, warm and comfortable in the feather bedding.

When Sorn came down the next morning, the steward was standing in the courtyard, laughing.

"Good morning, Sorn," he said. "How did you sleep last night?"

"Very comfortably, thank you," Sorn answered. "I like that room and I want to use it from now on."

"Didn't you notice anything . . . unusual?"

"Nothing but a flea in my leather breeches, and I took care of that in a hurry, believe me."

The steward didn't know what to make of this. So he said, "Today we're going to plough Long Ridge Field. I reckon we'll have to put eight ploughs on her. You can work one of them, can't you?"

"Yes, I can—two of them, for that matter," Sorn answered.

"Don't be foolish," the steward said. "How are you going to handle two ploughs at once?"

"Oh, I'm used to it," Sorn said. "With two ploughs I can do the work of eight. So you don't need to send anyone to help me."

"You must be daft!" the steward said. "We'll try it, but if you're bluffing the squire and me, we'll throw you out of Timsgaard."

"All right, that's my affair," Sorn said. "Now I must have matching horses—one team black and the other dun-coloured."

"Done!" The steward shook his head. "Well, what are you waiting for? Go and harness up!"

Sorn went inside and selected two of the best ploughs. He hitched them together, and in front of them he harnessed first the black horses and then the dun-coloured horses. The other carls ran along the side of the road, following Sorn to see what he would do. The steward and the squire joined them, and at last so many men were standing at the edge of Long Ridge Field that it was hard for Sorn to move past them. They all thought that he was mad.

Once out in the field, Sorn separated the ploughs and harnessed the black team to one and the dun team to the other. Then he whistled casually, as if to the horses. Immediately Tim shot up from the ground, but only Sorn could see him.

"Sweet porridge with butter for you; let's see what a nisse can do," Sorn said. "Can we plough the whole of Long Ridge Field by nightfall?"

The nisse burst out laughing.

"Help me up, and keep the pace!" he said, lifting his left leg up in the air. Sorn took hold of it and was about to help him up on the back of a black horse, but the nisse cried, "No, on the back of a dun-coloured horse!"

So Sorn had to do as he asked.

Hardly had the nisse mounted the horse when it let out a loud whinny and began to buck. It tossed Tim up in the air, nearly throwing him over its head. Tim caught hold of the horse's mane, slung his legs about its neck, and shouted angrily:

"I am from Morse!
My father could ride
a boar and a horse!"

With that he dug his little heels hard into the horse's nostrils and the horse reared. Sorn was sure that it would be the end of Tim, but suddenly he grew small as a mouse. In a flash he swung himself into the horse's left ear. All Sorn could see of Tim was the tip of his red cap. Then his head popped up. He nodded to Sorn and shouted:

"Steady now! Ready now!
Cleave the earth
with the plough!"

He cracked his tongue like a whip and yelled:

"Geehup! You tottering nag!
Geeho! You rickety mare!
I'll teach you critters
to pull your share!"

Tim's horses pulled and the soil rolled over the ploughshare as if the earth were sweet porridge. Sorn ran to his own plough and it began to move exactly like Tim's. The black horses pulled with such ease that when they had worked half an acre, they hadn't begun to sweat.

The other carls, who were still watching, marvelled at this. Each time the ploughs met, moving back and forth across the field, they heard a voice shout, "Hello, Sorn!" and Sorn answer, "Hello, Tim!" So they knew that something strange was going on, but they could not understand how the plough without a driver was cutting furrows just as deep and straight as Sorn's plough.

Towards afternoon the squire returned to see how the ploughing had progressed. To his astonishment he found the entire field finished and the horses still fresh.

"What a ploughman you are!" the squire shouted. "Normally it takes eight ploughs to turn over Long Ridge Field. What price are you asking for a day's work?"

"What shall I say?" Sorn whispered in the ear of the dun-coloured horse.

"Ask him for that," Tim said and pointed to a horse dropping fresh on the ground. "Then hand it up here to me."

"Master, if it doesn't offend you," Sorn said to the squire, "I should like to have that dropping there."

"Are you a fool?" the squire said. "If that's all you ask, take all the droppings in the field."

"Thank you, but one is enough," Sorn said. He tossed the dropping to Tim, who put it in his cap. To the squire he said, "May I unharness now?"

"By all means, unharness!" the squire replied. "You're the most worthy carl I've ever had. A pity you're such a dolt!"

That evening Sorn carried his own porridge up to the room. The kitchen maids had given him a big lump of newly churned butter, and he placed this in the middle of the porridge.

About midnight the nisse came, exactly as he had come the night before, but he groaned even more for he was carrying something heavy in his cap. He sat down to the porridge at once. When he had eaten it and licked his spoon, he said, "That was sweet porridge! And now it's your turn to be paid."

Tim emptied his cap onto Sorn's bed. As the dropping tumbled out, Sorn saw that it had turned to gold.

Sorn slept well that night.

The next morning after his breakfast Sorn went down to the courtyard, where he found the steward waiting for him. This time the Steward didn't laugh and he didn't ask how Sorn had slept. He glowered at Sorn and muttered, "Well, you won't be ploughing today. We have to thresh twenty-five loads of wheat by tomorrow morning. How many men will you need?"

"Oh, I think I can manage that much by myself," Sorn answered. "I've done it before."

"Like the very devil!" the steward exclaimed. "You must thresh with both ends of the flail." He handed the flailing-stick to Sorn.

"No, I thresh with both hands," Sorn said. "It's too slow with my left hand alone, and I may have to work part of the night, at that."

"Oh, work all night if you want!" the steward shouted. "But if you haven't threshed the twenty-five loads by sunrise, we'll toss you out on your ear!"

The steward went to the squire and told him that Sorn was such a dolt he claimed he could thresh twenty-five loads of wheat by sunrise all by himself.

"Well, if he can thresh as he can plough, he may be able to do it," the squire said. "Go down and ask him how much he wants for his labour."

Soon the steward returned and said that all Sorn wanted were the usual threshing wages, but that in reckoning these the chaff should be weighed with the grain.

"Oh, that can't amount to much," the squire said. "Tell him we'll weigh the chaff with the grain as he asks."

Sorn went into the barn. The other carls expected him to start work at once, but instead he wandered idly about, picked up a stalk of wheat here and a stalk there, rubbed the heads between his hands and blew off the husks. By noon he had threshed about an eighth of a barrel in this manner. Then he lay down in the straw and took a long nap. Late in the afternoon the squire came out and found Sorn still asleep.

"What do you think you're doing?" the squire shouted. "Those twenty-five loads of wheat must be threshed and ready for the stall-master to drive to the merchant's granary tomorrow morning, and here you are sleeping the afternoon away!"

"Master, if you will allow me a few more hours, the grain will be ready," Sorn said. "It's very hot in the afternoon and I have all the night."

"Are you going to thresh in the dark?" the squire asked.

"Yes, I'll have to because the night is dark," Sorn answered, "but after all, twenty-five loads are nothing. Each load can't amount to more than a few barrels full!"

He's as daft as they say, the squire thought, and although he was curious to see what would happen, he left Sorn alone in the barn.

When darkness set in, Sorn whistled and Tim appeared at once.

"Here are twenty-five loads of wheat. We must thresh them all before sunrise. What do you say?"

"Is that all?" Tim answered. "I haven't eaten my porridge yet, and I have some chores to do. I have to check up on the cow with the crooked horn to see that she doesn't reject her calf, and I have to make sure that the Tamstrup nisse hasn't been stealing from us again. In the meantime, you go up to the loft and start pitching the sheaves down. I'll come back and thresh them for you."

So Sorn went up and began pitching sheaves, but he grew more and more uneasy, for at midnight Tim had still not returned.

Then Sorn heard the wind start to howl across the pasture as if a storm were building up in the west. A clap of thunder shook the barn and the doors sprang open. Sorn nearly fell from the top loft, but he caught hold of a cross-beam just as a blast of wind rushed through the barn. Sheaves of grain flew about and the thatched roof rose up from the rafters. Sorn was so frightened that he swung himself up over the beam and clung to it with his arms and legs. It was as if the arms of a hundred windmills were racing through the barn—crashing, grinding, gnashing, whining—running wild before the storm. So much dust and chaff, and so many bits of straw swirled about that Sorn could hardly breathe; when he spread his fingers it felt as if the air were filled with cobwebs. All around him he heard the sound of wheat sheaves falling. A hundred threshers could have been at work for all the grain that rolled across the barn floor. In one corner he heard brooms sweeping the grain into piles, in another, pitchforks casting the straw up, and in the midst of all this commotion, a rough voice was roaring, keeping time with the beat of the flail:

"Sweat on the brow,
Helpers in kind!
Plenty's the work,
Scant is the time!"

All this went on for several hours. At the first sign of approaching dawn Sorn thought he could see something like a pendulum moving back and forth over his head.

"What's that?" he asked aloud.

Then he saw that it was the tassel of Tim's red cap swinging back and forth as he threshed. Tim was so big, that with his feet on the floor of the barn, the top of his cap brushed the cross-beams just under the roof. The flail he was swinging was as thick as a toll barrier, its handle as long as a haypole. It flew around in his hand as easily as if it were a willow whip.

Small grey nisser were hanging like swarms of rats over the beams, pitching sheaves of grain down to Tim. It was all they could do to keep up with him. The other end of the barn was alive with grey nisser, too. They were casting the straw up to the loft with pitchforks no bigger than kitchen forks. One of the grey nisser was too eager and he fell head-first from the highest loft. He screamed, and Sorn was sure he was done for, but the nisse plunged into the right-hand pocket of Tim's breeches. Only his feet stuck out, and they kicked pitifully for Tim didn't notice him and went on threshing.

"Hey, Tim! You'll squash him!" Sorn called. He reached out, but he grew dizzy and fell himself. He landed in a pile of grain up to his

waist, face to face with Tim. Tim was back to normal size and all the grey nisser had disappeared. The glow of dawn shone through the gable window and fell like a banner of dust across the inside of the barn.

"If only you were as handy with your hands as you are with your mouth," Tim said crossly, "we'd be finished now! You've spoiled it all! Now we shan't be able to separate the chaff and the grain before sunrise."

"What does it matter?" Sorn objected. "We're going to be paid for the weight of both the grain and the chaff!"

"That's right," Tim said, "but I do my work properly: the chaff separated from the grain. Their weights can be added together afterwards. Crawl up under the roof and make a hole in the thatching big enough to take a load of wheat. When you have done that, open all the shutters and both the doors. Then go outside and stand on the south side of the barn. There you won't risk getting caught in it."

Sorn didn't understand what the nisse meant; but he did as he was told, crawled up under the roof, and began to cut the thatching. The hole took him nearly an hour to make, and by the time he had opened the doors and walked to the south side of the barn, it was very light in the east, almost sunrise.

"At last!" Tim said. "We've no time to lose. Take hold of that old willow-tree. Don't look behind you, and don't concern yourself with what I'm doing."

Sorn took hold of the willow, but he couldn't resist glancing over his shoulder. He saw Tim shrink to the size of an ant and then quickly swell up like a monstrous cloud, hovering behind the barn. At the very peak of the roof his red cap was shimmering like fire. Tim's

face and beard were larger than the biggest load of wheat. Suddenly, Tim lowered his head, placed his mouth over the hole, and blew so hard he shook the willow-tree. The chaff flew out of the barn, eastward and westward, and all over the courtyard. The blast sounded more frightful than a huge clap of thunder. Windows sprang open and dogs howled. The carls rushed outside, bare except for their shirts; they thought that lightning had struck. The steward came too, wearing only one of his boots and with his whip in his hand.

"What in the devil's going on at this hour of the morning?" the squire shouted.

"It's only me. I'm winnowing the grain," Sorn said, "and I happened to sneeze, for my nose was stuffed up."

"Do you call that winnowing?" the squire demanded. "You've spread the chaff all over the place! The whole estate looks like a filthy pigsty."

"I'll sweep it up in no time," Sorn said, "if that's all that's bothering you, Master." He ran back to the willow-tree and asked Tim to help him.

"You breathe out and I'll breathe in," Tim said. "Run three times around the courtyard, you go this way and I'll go that way."

With that, the nisse ran in one direction and Sorn in the other, Tim inhaling and Sorn exhaling. Together they blew up such a whirlwind that it swept the chaff into the middle of the courtyard and whipped it into a pile almost as big as a haystack.

"Now that's done," Sorn said, "and it's time to weigh the chaff and the grain."

"I think this carl has a pact with a demon," mused the squire. "If we weigh the chaff with the wheat, he'll get much more than the usual threshing wages."

"But, Master, you promised me that yourself!" Sorn said. "Surely you will not go against your word?"

"Oh, yes, I will!" the squire said. "I'd be out of my mind to pay you more than others get."

"But I can do more than others!" Sorn answered.

"What can you do?" the squire asked. "Bellow like a bull! Others can do that, too."

"If you don't pay me according to your promise, I'll leave," Sorn said. "But first I'll knock down your barn."

"Go right ahead! Do just that!" the squire answered. "If you can even rock it, I'll pay you at once. Apparently you don't know timber from Norway."

"Nay, but we grow timber in Jutland, too," Sorn said. He walked over to the barn and set his shoulder to the wall.

"Yow! What was that?" the carls shouted.

It looked as if flames were shooting up from the peak of the roof. Tim's cap was poking through the hole in the thatching; he had set his shoulders against the rafters and was lifting the entire roof-ridge. Chalk and gravel rained down. The walls cracked and the barn began to tremble as if there were an earthquake.

"Halt, stop!" the squire shouted. "That carl is pushing the barn down on our heads. Set your price, carl."

"Keep your side of the bargain!" Sorn answered, and moved away from the barn. At that moment the sun appeared over the horizon and the barn stood as steady as before.

The weighing began, and it seemed as if it would never end. Whenever the carls shovelled a load of chaff into the barn, Tim carried it out again in his cap, grown as big as a barrel. Not until evening did they finish the work and find that Sorn had earned five hundred daler for threshing the wheat. He took these with him up to the nisse's room and laid them away with the gold horse dropping. Together they came to a pretty sum.

The next day the squire said to the steward, "I'm afraid that head-carl is beset by some demon. If we throw him out, he may take revenge. The best way to get rid of him is to pay him a week's wages and give him no work to do. Then he'll leave of his own accord."

Instead of leaving, Sorn settled down to enjoy his leisure. One night after he had spent all day sunning himself, Tim came in late. "The cow with the crooked horn won't have anything to do with her calf," he said. "This is the third one she's rejected. She's never given any milk. I think you should buy her."

"Why should I buy that dried-up old critter?" Sorn asked. "She's no good at all."

"That's why you should buy her. The squire will sell her for next to nothing, and then I'll teach you to deal with cattle."

Sorn bought the cow and the squire bet him one hundred daler that he couldn't make any money on her. So, although it was thirty miles to market and the cow looked as if she couldn't drag herself more than ten, Sorn and Tim started off that very evening. As they walked, the cow began sniffling and stumbling.

"Look how she's sinking down in her knees," Sorn said.

"Ay, she's not much for dancing," Tim observed. "She looks almost as if her heart's been broken."

"She can't walk much farther."

"Neither can I," Tim said. "So I'll ride her."

"Ride her! You're not going to ride that sorry wretch!"

Tim took a backwards jump and landed on the cow. He grabbed her tail as if it were reins and shouted, "Hip, hip! Get moving, you crooked-horned beast!" He dug his heels into her bony buttocks and the cow moved, first at a walk and then at a gallop. She left the road, crossed the meadow, and went to the middle of the alder swamp where grasses shone like silver in the moonlit mist.

"This is where the elves danced tonight," Tim said. "We'll leave her here to graze until morning, and we'll sleep in the haystack there."

An odd thing to do, Sorn thought, for he had always heard that where elves had danced, cattle took ill. He said nothing though, and with Tim, he lay down to sleep in the hay.

They woke up at dawn and saw the cow lying in the middle of the swamp, shaking all over as if she had ague. She was more dead than alive.

Tim took a handful of the hay on which he had slept. He climbed up on the back of the cow and began to rub her with it. Sorn could hardly believe his eyes; each time Tim rubbed the cow with the wisp of hay, she grew fatter and fatter. When the nisse had finished his work, she was the stoutest cow to reach the market. If it hadn't been for her crooked horn—Tim couldn't straighten that—she would have brought a fancy price. Still, they sold her to Kresten Kren and Sorn couldn't complain, for with that money, and the squire's, too, he was two hundred and ten daler the richer.

Not long after that, the squire called Sorn to him and said, "You're not as foolish as you seem. I want to make you a proposition. For some time I've known that my steward is a clod, but this morning I discovered in my accounts that he is a cheat as well. If you will promise to serve me honestly and to look after the best interests of the manor, I will make you my steward in his stead, for luck seems to be with you."

Thus Sorn became steward of Timsgaard, and it was remarkable how the manor thrived from that day on. The horses stood strong and well-groomed in the stalls, the cows gave milk, and the hens laid eggs as never before. The barn was filled to the collar-beam with grain to be threshed, and even though twenty-five threshers worked for thirty days, the supply didn't diminish. The squire told Sorn he was afraid they wouldn't finish the threshing at all that year.

One evening Tim entered the barn through the kitty-hole, which was there for the manor cats. He was dragging a sheaf of wheat no bigger than a bread loaf, but he was gasping for breath as if he were dragging an immense burden.

"Out of breath carrying a little load like that?" Sorn said. "If that's all you can carry, you shouldn't bother. Anyway, we have enough."

"Enough is never too much," Tim answered. "A fine steward you are, upbraiding your squire's helper. You don't see very well, do you? Come with me. I'll show you!"

Tim went back out of the kitty-hole and stamped across the stone bridge. Sorn followed him. When they reached the heath, Tim made himself bigger so as not to get lost in the heather. The moonlight was bright enough for Sorn to make out his red cap darting here and there among the heather clumps like a lightning bug.

"Where are we going?" Sorn asked.

"To Tamstrup Manor," the nisse said. "Keep up with me because I'm going to move fast."

"Be careful you don't run your legs off," Sorn said, but he regretted having said it because it angered Tim into moving so fast he looked like a red wheel racing down the road. Sorn had to run to keep him in sight. At last, and quite out of breath, he reached Tamstrup Manor, nearly three miles away. The dogs growled and howled when they heard Sorn running and they frightened Tim so much he rolled into the ditch and hid himself in a culvert.

"Come here!" he motioned to Sorn. Sorn jumped into the ditch, but he was much too big to hide in the culvert, even on all fours.

"Bite this!" Tim said. He plucked a tansy plant from the edge of the ditch.

"Foy! It puckers the mouth!" Sorn said. As he tasted the bitter herb he felt his whole body shrinking, shrinking until he fitted easily

inside the culvert, which looked like the vault of a church with dandelion chandeliers.

"Move along! Farther in!" Tim whispered. At the other end of the culvert they came to a tall archway covered with an iron grating. It was the drain from the Tamstrup barn.

"Jump on, jump on!" Tim said, pointing to two brown animals. Sorn jumped on but he thought their steeds looked suspiciously like rats. They galloped right up the hill and into the barn.

"Take some.
Keep mum,"

Tim said. Here and there he picked up a piece of straw as he walked across the barn floor. Sorn noticed that he chose those with the heaviest heads. So he copied Tim. At the south end of the barn they both went out through the kitty-hole; it seemed as big as a barn door. They stopped to look at the moonlight and for a moment Sorn thought that the Tamstrup Chapel was a mountain. Later, when he met an ant on the road, he tipped his hat to it. They crossed the meadow. The grass towered above their heads, and a snail falling from a dockweed leaf nearly knocked Sorn down. As they walked on, Sorn began to feel normal, and by the time they reached Long Ridge it occurred to him that he was once again the carl he had always been. He wondered why those few stalks of grain weighed so heavily on his shoulders. He was bent under their weight as he walked up the ridge.

Behind him he heard Tim moan, "Ay, vay! Ay, vok! These three stalks of grain are at fault if we never get over Long Ridge."

"Let's sit down and take a rest."

"Rest, what's rest?" Tim gasped.

"Oh, it's sitting down, casting off your burden, and stretching your limbs!" Sorn said and threw himself in the grass. That very moment he heard a noise like a whole load of hay tipping over.

"Whew," Tim said, "it feels good. I've never tried this before. Rest and I are going to be good friends!" When they were ready to move again, Tim said, "Sorn, if I had known rest and how good he is, I would have taken everything in the Tamstrup barn!"

Sorn turned around. Then he saw the load of grain on Tim's back, as big as a haystack. He couldn't even see the nisse underneath it, but the stack was moving slowly down the ridge directly towards Timsgaard. Sorn had to open both the barn doors in order to get the load in, and at last he understood why twenty-five threshers couldn't finish the harvest. Each time they threshed a barrelful Tim brought in two new loads!

One evening Sorn went down to see if Tim had brought in another load. Sure enough, Sorn found him sitting astride a barrel.

"Good evening, Tim!" Sorn said. "Are we going out again tonight?"

The small grey man looked up and said, "If you take Tam for Tim, greet Tim from Tam. Tell Tim if Tim takes from Tam, then Tam takes from Tim!" With that he disappeared.

"Strange mumble-jumble!" Sorn thought, and he knew he hadn't been talking to Tim. That night in the nisse's room, when he heard the spoon stirring the porridge, he said offhandedly, "Tam is in Timsgaard!"

"What did you say! Tam in Timsgaard! Confound him! Let calamity befall him!" Tim screamed and smacked the spoon in the porridge so hard that he splashed butter all over the room. "Come with me, we'll get him!"

Sorn and Tim went down to the barn. No one was in sight, but it seemed to Sorn that there were fewer sheaves on the racks at the south end than had been there that morning. He mentioned this to Tim.

"We must leave at once!" Tim said. They went to Tamstrup Manor as they had gone before. This time, though, Sorn was careful not to take too many stalks, but Tim took even more. On the way home Tim grew short of breath and began to pant. During the climb up Long Ridge he said, "Now I think it's time for rest, and I'm glad because tonight I have taken almost everything in the barn."

Sorn turned around and saw that Tim was carrying a load even larger than the biggest haystack. He puffed and panted and toiled away. Just as they reached the top of the ridge they met another stack coming up from the other side. Before Sorn could say a word the two stacks ran into each other and two nisser fell on their noses.

"It's Tam!" Tim shouted.

"Yes, it's Tam!" Tam yelled.

The nisser went at each other with straw sticking out of their ears. The fight was murderous. They pulled each other's hats off and trampled on them. They hit each other on the nose and mouth. They tore and scratched and screamed and spat and snarled as if they were a hundred cats. Tam kicked Tim in the stomach and Tim shouted to high heaven. He had to sit on a stone and be sick.

Meanwhile, Tam crept in under his load and started down the ridge, but Tim raced after him, yelling, "Sorn, help me! Where's something to hit him with?"

"There's a plough over there," Sorn said.

Tim grabbed the plough, swung it over his head, and walloped Tam with it. Tam and his load went rolling down the ridge.

"That was a splendid blow!" Sorn said as he watched Tam limp away across the field.

There were two harrows at the foot of the ridge and the minute Tam saw them he took one in each hand and raced back up the hill like a wind-storm. He smacked Tim with both harrows at once. The teeth of the harrows went right through him and he was stuck fast between them.

"Pick me out! Pick me out!" Tim screamed. Quickly Sorn pulled the two harrows apart. Tim wept. Oh, what a sight he was! He was so full of holes that Sorn could see right through him as if he were a colander. Three of his ribs were broken, too, but what angered Tim most of all was the sight of a limping Tam, getting away with his load.

"Carry me home and put me to bed," Tim whimpered. "Rub me down with mosquito fat and bring me a spider for lunch. Then I'll be fit to return the hospitality of that Tamstrup nisse!"

Sorn carried Tim home and cared for him well. The next morning no one on the estate could understand why two harrows were on the top of Long Ridge or why the rick of wheat at the south end of the barn had disappeared.

After that night Sorn noticed that the stock of wheat in the barn was dwindling. The threshers were catching up with the supply. He didn't dare tell Tim about it because Tim was so miserable and despondent that he could hardly eat his porridge, much less deal with the Tamstrup nisse.

In time, the holes closed and Tim grew more spirited. One evening after they had gone to bed, Tim limped over to Sorn and asked how things were going. Sorn had to confess. When Tim heard that the grain was disappearing, he sat down and cried tears as big as sparrow eggs. They rolled right into Sorn's bed.

"There, there, it's nothing to cry about," Sorn said. "Your luck will be better next time."

"Luck? What is luck?" Tim asked.

"It's like something moving round and round on the rim of a wheel," Sorn said. "Sometimes up and sometimes down. Next time you'll come up on top."

A few weeks later, just as Sorn was about to close the door to the barn for the night, he was surprised to see Tim scurrying from one rack to another. He looked worried when he said to Sorn, "I've counted every sheaf in the barn. That nisse Tam has taken just as much grain from us as we took from him. If this continues, he'll ruin us!"

"Someone ought to break his neck," Sorn said. "Can't you get rid of him?"

"No," Tim said, "I can't—unless you help me. My side hurts too much when I move my right arm."

"Tell me what to do and I will help you!" Sorn said.

Tim climbed up on a rack, sat down, and crossed his legs. He spoke slowly. "What you saw on Long Ridge was mere child's play compared with what's coming. We nisser cannot ruin one another in our own form, but if we take another form we can fight for life and death. Tonight Tam will come to Timsgaard. We must make sure that we have luck and come up on top. I'll turn myself into a wheel with nine spokes, and he'll turn into one with twelve. He broke three of mine up on Long Ridge. When you see the two wheels collide you must take a muck-rake and strike the spokes of the big wheel until every last one of them breaks. If you don't succeed, it will be the end of Tim."

Sorn wanted to learn more, but Tim disappeared and he didn't even show up for his porridge that evening. Then Sorn knew that something very serious was about to happen. Towards midnight Sorn slipped quietly down to the barn with a sturdy muck-rake in his hand. The moment the watchman cried twelve in the courtyard, the doors of the barn flew open and out rolled a small, glowing wheel with nine spokes. The sight of its flashing made Sorn feel strange. At the same time he heard a huge crash behind the barn. A big white, glowing wheel came rolling around the corner and rammed the little wheel. The little wheel lost a spoke and rolled into the ditch. Sorn was so frightened that he forgot to strike, but the little wheel recovered speedily, rolled out of the ditch, and struck back at the big one, knocking two of its spokes out. As if they were in a spinning race, the two wheels whirled around each other, flaming and shooting sparks. The flames shot up so high that Sorn was fearful of their setting fire to the barn.

Suddenly the little wheel took such a blow that it flew straight into the water trough and there it floated, sputtering and sizzling. It had lost another spoke.

"I must do something now," Sorn thought. He waded into the trough, fished the wheel up with the muck-rake, and tossed it on to the ground.

Immediately the big wheel threw itself at the little one and hammered and mauled it mercilessly. Sorn swung the muck-rake at the big wheel and he broke two more of its spokes. It crackled, turned and rushed at Sorn's legs, singeing his breeches and burning his skin.

"Oh, so you're looking for trouble!" Sorn shouted. He lashed out at the hub of the big wheel and all the spokes broke loose. The little wheel raced with all its might into the battle again. It rammed the big wheel and sent the loose spokes flying in every direction. Sorn struck again and the big wheel flew over the roof of the barn. In mid-air it broke into twelve pieces that sailed through the darkness like balls of fire, each with a glowing tail after it. These burned out one by one. Then Sorn heard a voice in the dark:

"Now Tam from Tamstrup's dead!
And Tim's still fresh and red!
The luck of Timsgaard's up."

He saw Tim wring water out of his cap, for he was still a bit moist from lying in the water trough.

After that night, life at Timsgaard went on as usual. Prosperity showed in the barn, in the stable, in the byre, and in the chicken coop. The squire rejoiced over his blessings, seeing that there was more than enough of everything; but he made one grave mistake. He believed that Timsgaard was thriving because he himself handled the affairs of the manor so well. Whenever Sorn mentioned the nisse, the squire laughed and said "Nonsense!"

Sorn disliked this ingratitude. So, when he had served for a few years and had become good friends with the milkmaid, he went to the squire and asked for a land-holding. He had saved enough money to become a freeman.

"I am sorry to see you go," the squire said. "You have been my steward for three years now and they have been good years."

"It's not to my credit, Master," Sorn said. "If the nisse had not been with me, we would never have done this well."

"Oh, the devil is plaguing you with that nisse!" the squire said. "*I* have never seen him."

"If I may have the holding, I will let you see him, Master, just this once," Sorn said.

"How can you manage that?" the squire asked.

"Tonight, at twelve o'clock, you must climb the spiral staircase in the east tower and peek through the keyhole in the door at the top of the stairs. I'll arrange for you to see him."

That night when Tim had eaten his porridge, Sorn said, "Now you must do me a favour for having pulled you out of the water trough. You must take off your cap when the watchman cries twelve."

"Why so?"

"Well, the squire wants to have a look at you, and I have given him permission to peek through the keyhole."

"I don't like that!" Tim said. "Still, if you have promised him, I'll do it this once. A curse on him if he ever tries it again."

At twelve o'clock that night the squire crept up the tower stairs to the door of the room and peeked through the key-hole. He saw a little old, bow-legged man with a big, uncombed beard sitting on a chair, repairing his breeches. The squire thought it was the cowherd and said so to Sorn the next morning, but the cowherd claimed that he had been asleep in the byre at midnight and the other carls vouched for him.

So, although the squire wasn't satisfied with the nisse he had seen, for he had expected someone very different, he had to give Sorn the holding.

"Tell me," the squire said when Sorn was ready to leave, "if it's true what you say, how did you and the nisse become good friends?"

"It was because of my leather breeches," Sorn replied. "He wanted them so badly that I let him try them on."

Sorn got his farm, and a wife besides, and they did fairly well. Timsgaard was as prosperous as ever and the squire was then sure that the manor's good fortune was not due to Sorn.

In November he employed a new housekeeper who couldn't be

bothered carrying porridge up the many stairs to the nisse's room; so she didn't do it. This angered Tim and from that day on the affairs of Timsgaard took a turn for the worse. The barn burned down, the cattle grew ill, and one morning the squire's favourite mare was found dead in the stable.

The squire began to wonder what was the cause of his troubles. Remembering the night he had seen the nisse sewing patches on his old breeches and mindful of what Sorn had told him, he decided he should give the nisse a new pair of breeches. So, just before Christmas, he went to the town and engaged the best tailor to sew a pair of durable leather breeches with shiny buttons and a reliable rope-clamp.

On Christmas Eve he had the breeches placed on the chair in the nisse's room, but both he and the housekeeper forgot to set out the nisse's Christmas porridge.

As midnight approached the squire thought of going to bed, but it occurred to him that it might be fun to see what the nisse thought of his new breeches. Quietly he climbed up the spiral staircase and placed his eye against the key-hole of the door. He saw the nisse dressed for travel with a walking stick in his hand and a bundle under his arm. The new leather breeches lay untouched on the chair.

The squire exclaimed, "I think he's forgetting his breeches!"

The nisse grabbed the breeches and flung them so hard against the door that one of the buttons blackened the squire's eye. Then he disappeared from Timsgaard and no one there ever saw him again.

That same night Sorn and his wife were preparing to go to bed after spending their first Christmas Eve together. "Even though we are very fortunate, wife," Sorn said, "I have a strange feeling that something is missing."

"What can that be?" she asked.

"Well, you needn't feel jealous, wife, but at bedtime I miss the Timsgaard nisse with whom I shared the tower room."

"Oh, I think you're crazy, husband!" his wife said. She snuffed out the candle and settled down in bed.

As she did so, the front door opened and closed again. Someone moved towards the wall bench and it sounded as if that someone put down a bundle.

"What is it, Sorn? Do you think the house is haunted, or is it only the cat?"

"Nay, it's not the cat. I know the ways of my friend. In a minute you'll see him."

Sorn grabbed the iron from the tinder-box and tossed it towards the bench. It flared up and his wife saw a little old man wiping his brow with his cap.

"Tim, it's you!" Sorn called out. "What are you doing here?"

"I don't like living at Timsgaard any more," the nisse answered, "and I'm never going back."

"Why not?"

"Because they tease me. Tonight I was looking forward to my Christmas porridge but when I got home, that misbegotten squire had left nothing for me but a pair of leather breeches. Now I'm going to stay with you and I want my Christmas porridge!"

Sorn's wife brought out the porridge, and the nisse helped himself to a whopping portion. "Ah, that was porridge," he said and licked the spoon.

"On this land I set my stake,
Fortune grow and joy be great."

And he kept his word. Sorn and his wife came into wealth and happiness.

Timsgaard, on the other hand, declined rapidly and the buildings fell into disrepair and crumbled. Finally the manor house was torn down, and since then the west wind has had free play over the moat.